Mark

Living the Way of Jesus in the World

A six-session Bible study for individuals and small groups

By Tracy Cotterell

licc.

'But what about you?' he asked.
'Who do you say I am?'
Peter answered,
'You are the Messiah.'

Mark 8:29

INTER-VARSITY PRESS
36 Causton Street, London SW1P 4ST, England
Email: ivp@ivpbooks.com
Website: www.ivpbooks.com

First published 2021

British Library Cataloguing-in-Publication Data
A catalogue record for this book is available from the British Library

Paperback ISBN: 9781789743661
Ebook ISBN: 9781789743678

Typeset in Great Britain by Mark Steel
Illustrations by Michael Ridley
Printed in Great Britain by Ashford Colour Press Ltd., Gosport, Hampshire

Inter-Varsity Press publishes Christian books that are true to the
Bible and that communicate the gospel, develop discipleship,
and strengthen the church for its mission in the world.

IVP originated within the Inter-Varsity Fellowship, now the
Universities and Colleges Christian Fellowship, a student movement
connecting Christian Unions in universities and colleges throughout
Great Britain, and a member movement of the International
Fellowship of Evangelical Students. Website: www.uccf.org.uk.
That historic association is maintained, and all senior IVP staff
and committee members subscribe to the UCCF Basis of Faith.

Contents

Features

The Gateway Seven

Exodus — Law

Ezekiel — Prophecy

Mark — Gospel

1 Peter — Letters

Proverbs — Wisdom

Revelation — Apocalyptic

Ruth — Narrative

The Gateway Seven Bible Study Series

We don't approach a novel in the same way we tackle a legal document. We don't read poetry in the same way we might read a letter from a friend. So, we don't read the 66 books of the Bible as if they were all the same kind of writing. Story, song, law, letter, and more, all make up the rich repository of writing that together is God's word to us.

For *The Gateway Seven* series we've selected seven books of the Bible that each represent a different kind of writing. The mini-features sprinkled through the studies, together with the questions suggested for discussion, invite you to explore each book afresh in a way that's sensitive to its genre as well as to the concerns of the book itself.

Each study engages with a different kind of writing. However, each one in the series has been crafted with the same central desire: to offer a gateway to a deeper love of God's word and richer insights into its extraordinary implications for all of life, Monday through Sunday.

'May your kingdom come – on earth as in heaven', Jesus taught us to pray. May your kingdom come in our homes and places of work and service. May your kingdom come at the school gate as well as in the sanctuary. May your kingdom come in the hydrotherapy pool, in the council chamber, on the estate, around the Board table. May your kingdom come as we learn to live our everyday lives as beloved sons and daughters, wondrously wrapped up in our Father's 'family business'.

Our prayer is that these seven distinctive books of the Bible will be a gateway for you to a richer, deeper, transforming life with God wherever you are – seven days a week.

Tracy Cotterell
The Gateway Seven Series Editor
Senior Mission Associate
LICC

Making the Most of Mark

Introduction to Mark
Living the Way of Jesus in the World

───

'The beginning of the gospel about Jesus the Messiah, the Son of God' (1:1).

The Gospel of Mark is stunning. From its opening declaration heralding an astounding new move of God, right through to its somewhat surprising ending, Mark leaves us in no doubt that this is the greatest story ever told, one that changed the world forever.

There was a time when Mark's Gospel was overshadowed by the seemingly more orderly and fuller versions from Matthew, Luke, and John. Today, however, Mark's skills as a writer and his depth as a theologian have come to the fore. Generally considered the earliest of the four Gospels, Mark's gospel-telling is recognised as the work of a true craftsman who also knew Israel's Scriptures intimately. He was a consummate storyteller who wrote to be heard

rather than read, his style making it easy for his listeners to follow the flow and to pass the story on.

The author is traditionally identified as the John Mark of Acts (Acts 12:12, 25). Tradition also connects the Gospel's origins with the apostle Peter. Writing at the beginning of the second century, Papias, Bishop of Hierapolis, recorded a certain Mark, Peter's secretary and translator, writing up all that he had heard from Peter about Jesus. Mark's vivid and profound account certainly bears the hallmarks of someone who was at the heart of the first-century church.

It is, of course, Jesus himself who is front and centre of Mark's Gospel. Who is this Jesus? What has God done through Jesus that changes everything? What does it mean to follow him? These, and more, are the questions we can bring to Mark's Gospel. He will not disappoint.

Imagine Mark as one who had longed for the fulfilment of God's promises to his people. Imagine him hearing the revolutionary story of Jesus and starting to make sense of it in the light of all that God had done over the centuries, all he had signposted through his prophets. Imagine him gripped by the loving faithfulness of God in Jesus.

Imagine Mark in the context of a persecuted early church. Imagine him seeing Jesus-followers who lived and sometimes died for one who had transformed their lives and hopes. Imagine him learning about Jesus: radical, humble, authoritative, joyous, unpredictable, compassionate, confrontational, suffering servant. Imagine him overwhelmed by the sacrificial love of God in Jesus, God's Son.

It's not difficult then to imagine Mark inspired by the Spirit to capture this Jesus-story, this good-news-God story, in the best way he knew how so that others might trust King Jesus completely, surrendering to him joyfully as Lord of all.

There are lots of ways to read Mark's Gospel. You can read it quickly, caught up in the energy, urgency, and directness of Mark's telling. You can read it slowly, reaping the rewards of paying attention to the ways Mark wants you to grasp this good news of Jesus Christ in all its fullness.

There will be implications. Whatever you discover these to be for you and the frontlines where God has placed you, may the way, the truth, and the life of Jesus revealed in Mark's Gospel inspire you to trust him in all things, always.

For a great overview of the Gospel of Mark, together with other free, short videos on key themes in the story of Jesus, go to **bibleproject.com**

Studying Mark

———

This Bible study is designed to look at select passages in the Gospel of Mark over six sessions:

Session 1 | **Announcing Revolution** (Mark 1:1-15)

Session 2 | **Demonstrating Authority** (Mark 4:35-41)

Session 3 | **Revealing Identity** (Mark 8:27-38)

Session 4 | **Challenging Allegiance** (Mark 10:17-31)

Session 5 | **Transforming Power** (Mark 14:32-52)

Session 6 | **Inviting Trust** (Mark 16:1-8)

You can work through each session on your own, one-to-one, or in a small group.

If your church's preaching programme is covering the Gospel of Mark, this study is a really helpful way to deepen your understanding of the book and explore its implications for Monday to Saturday life. Working through the sessions in a group is also a great opportunity to encourage one another with insights and stories of how you've seen God at work in your own context.

Each group has its own way of doing things, so the session plan is only a suggestion, not a rule.

Suggested session plan

1 Pray to open

2 Read the 'First Thoughts' section

3 Read the passage from Mark

4 Work through the questions

They cover the session's main theme, what the Bible passage says and means, going deeper, and living out the passage. Many questions don't have 'right' or 'wrong' answers. It's important and helpful to hear insights from others. Naturally, group leaders may want to pick out the most pertinent questions for their group to discuss.

5 Pray to close

Don't feel bound by the prayer prompts if your study has taken a different turn. Be flexible in responding to each other's needs.

You'll see that we've included five brief feature pieces on questions or issues related to the background and study of Mark. Together with some real-life stories – lived examples of how God's word can be worked out in daily life – they offer insights to deepen our understanding of the book and its implications.

We've changed the names of the people in the stories and some details to preserve their anonymity.

Participating in the study

Before the first session

Mark is one whole story, so it would be great to read or listen to the Gospel in
one sitting before you start the study. You'll need a couple of hours for this but
there are different ways you could do it. Of course, you could find a corner and
read it, with the odd beverage break along the way. Perhaps you might listen
to it on your commute. Or maybe you'd like to watch it being read by David
Suchet with a friend or your group – find it at **stpauls.co.uk/marksgospel**.
For a one-man, word-for-word dramatisation of the Gospel, check out
iam-mark.com

Take a moment, too, to think about your frontline using the
questions on the next page. They may help you discern the way
of Jesus in your everyday life as you explore Mark's Gospel.

Each session

Before each session, you might like to read the passage, together with
one of the features and any explanation boxes or stories that accompany
it. As you respond to each session in prayer, ask God to bring to mind
someone you'd love to draw closer to Jesus. Keep a note of who you
pray for and how God answers your prayers. After you meet, you
could pursue some of the 'Going Deeper' questions on your own.

Alongside the study

You may want to read through the whole of Mark more slowly on
your own. There's a suggested reading guide on pages 16-17.

> Another way to experience the whole of Mark's Gospel is to join LICC's
> digital devotional journey. This is a series of daily readings through Mark's
> Gospel delivered through email or the YouVersion Bible app.
> Sign up at **licc.org.uk/mark-devotional**.

My frontline

Your frontline is an everyday place where you live, work, study, or play and where you're likely to connect with people who aren't Christians. Before you start the study, reflect on your frontline using these questions.

Where is your frontline?

What do you do there?

Who's there?

What's going on at the moment?

What are you excited about or struggling with?

What opportunities for making an impact for Christ do you see in and through what you do and who you connect with?

Come back to this reflection throughout the sessions, praying and trusting that God will direct your ways through his word.

Outline of Mark's Gospel

Many have found it helpful to read Mark as if it were a drama in three acts. You can use this outline to guide your reading alongside the study. The passages highlighted in red indicate the readings for the six study sessions. Use the questions to prompt reflection on each passage.

- What does it say about who God is?

- What does it say about how God works?

- What are the implications for us as God's people?

- What insights does it offer for our frontlines?

- What prayers does it prompt?

1:1–15	**Prologue** Announcing revolution

Act 1
In and around Galilee – Who is Jesus?

1:16–34	Calling the disciples; exorcism
1:35–2:12	Healings
2:13–22	Controversy and conflict
2:23–3:12	Lord of the Sabbath
3:13–35	Calling the Twelve; insiders and outsiders
4:1–34	Parables about the kingdom of God
4:35–41	Demonstrating authority
5:1–43	Mighty deeds 1
6:1–29	Controversy and conflict
6:30–56	Mighty deeds 2
7:1–23	Teaching on purity
7:24–8:21	Mighty deeds 3; growing tension

Act 2
On the way to Jerusalem - Discipleship

———

Act 3
In Jerusalem - What did Jesus come to do?

———

What are the Gospels?

Genre, or the kind of writing we understand a book to be, signposts how we're expected to read it. So, what are the Gospels?

In Greek, the word 'gospel' is *euangelion*. The word was in common use in the first century to describe an important announcement. It heralded news that should be celebrated. So, people in the first-century Roman Empire would be accustomed to hearing *euangelion*, good news, about Caesar's exploits and achievements. 'Gospel' is also an Old Testament word used by the prophets to announce the liberation of God's people from exile or oppression (Isaiah 61:1-2).

Justin Martyr, the second-century Christian philosopher, referred to the Gospels as *euangelia* (plural): Gospels. He called them 'memoirs' about the life of Jesus. Origen, another early Christian scholar, described them as 'histories' or 'investigations'. At one time, most scholars considered the Gospels to be a unique genre of their own, created by Mark who is now generally agreed to be the earliest Gospel-writer. In recent times, many scholars have seen that the Gospels fit well with an ancient form of biography, *bios*. This makes sense in that the 'Gospels' are all about the life and death of Jesus.

But ancient biographies shouldn't be seen in the same way as modern biographies. Today, we expect lots of insights into a person through their biography that the ancients didn't – detail about the subject's childhood and psychological insights into their personality and motivation, for example. Ancient biographies weren't interested in such things. Rather, their interest lay in instructing readers about the subject's life as a way of life to follow. They were worthy subjects to imitate, to learn from, and the author wanted people to grasp this. Such biographies were often written about someone who played a central role in history at the time.

The subject of the Gospels, Jesus Christ, is unique. His coming marked a radical new move of God in history, and different Gospel authors recount this in different ways. Whilst the literary form of ancient biography is likely to have been familiar to the early church, the Gospels were nevertheless distinctive in their biblical roots and teaching about Jesus.

In our Bibles, the four Gospels form the beginning of the New Testament. They're clearly not the beginning of God's dealings with people and the world. Rather, they continue a story that had begun long ago but which now finds its climax and fulfilment in Jesus of Nazareth. Mark, through his many references and allusions to the Old Testament, encourages us to read the story of Jesus within this larger story.

Matthew, Mark, and Luke are sometimes referred to as the synoptic Gospels – synoptic meaning 'seen together' because they tell many of the same stories. Mark's Gospel differs in some ways from the other two. There's no account of Jesus' birth. The disciples are portrayed as particularly confused and uncomprehending. Jesus frequently stops people from speaking about what he's done – it's rather odd for someone who's announcing 'good news'. His message is subversive, deliberately overturning expectations. Mark also differs from John's Gospel with its alternative portfolio of stories and extensive discourses of Jesus, though both Gospels share a concern for deep reflection on the person and purposes of God.

Four Gospels. Four windows on the life and ministry of Jesus, written for different reasons and audiences. All pointing to the one good news announcement – the coming of Jesus the King.

Session 1

Announcing Revolution

Mark 1:1–15

First Thoughts

In a game of word association, I say 'revolution' and you might respond 'conflict' or 'coup' – or 'guillotine' if you've recently watched *Les Misérables*. 'Revolution' is a word calculated to shock. It was British theologian David Wenham who proposed 'The revolution is here!' as a contemporary equivalent for Jesus' announcement of the 'kingdom of God'. He was driving at the heart of Jesus' message: God was taking over in a new way. God was working out his purposes. God was in control.

'Kingdom' is a common word in Christian circles today. Understandably, perhaps, we rarely experience the thrill those first followers felt when they heard Jesus' proclamation. But the arrival of Jesus the Nazarene on the scene in first-century Galilee, declaring that Israel's long-held hopes for God's kingship were about to be realised, was as disruptive as it was dramatic.

Of course, Jesus failed to conform to expectations. Forever faithful, God would indeed fulfil his promise to his people. Through Jesus, he would be God with them once more. Uniquely unpredictable, God would radically reveal that his ways in the world truly weren't theirs. Through Jesus, God was indeed doing a new thing. This was news, and it was very good.

So, as we fix our eyes on Jesus with the help of the Gospel-writer, let's allow Mark's opening scenes to stir us into seeing Jesus with fresh eyes. May the Spirit refresh our wonder at the coming of the King and provoke us to consider our own response to him again.

Read – Mark 1:1–15

¹The beginning of the good news about
Jesus the Messiah, the Son of God, ² as
it is written in Isaiah the prophet:

'I will send my messenger ahead of you,
who will prepare your way'—
³ 'a voice of one calling in the wilderness,
"Prepare the way for the Lord,
make straight paths for him."'

⁴ And so John the Baptist appeared in the
wilderness, preaching a baptism of repentance
for the forgiveness of sins. ⁵ The whole Judean
countryside and all the people of Jerusalem
went out to him. Confessing their sins, they were
baptised by him in the River Jordan. ⁶ John wore
clothing made of camel's hair, with a leather
belt round his waist, and he ate locusts and wild
honey. ⁷ And this was his message: 'After me
comes the one more powerful than I, the straps
of whose sandals I am not worthy to stoop
down and untie. ⁸ I baptise you with water,
but he will baptise you with the Holy Spirit.'

⁹ At that time Jesus came from Nazareth in Galilee and was baptised by John in the Jordan. ¹⁰ Just as Jesus was coming up out of the water, he saw heaven being torn open and the Spirit descending on him like a dove. ¹¹ And a voice came from heaven: 'You are my Son, whom I love; with you I am well pleased.'

¹² At once the Spirit sent him out into the wilderness, ¹³ and he was in the wilderness for forty days, being tempted by Satan. He was with the wild animals, and angels attended him.

¹⁴ After John was put in prison, Jesus went into Galilee, proclaiming the good news of God. ¹⁵ 'The time has come,' he said. 'The kingdom of God has come near. Repent and believe the good news!'

Focus on the Theme

1. Can you recall a time when something wonderful and unexpected happened to you? Briefly share with one another, describing how you felt and how you responded.

What Does the Bible Say?

2. John the Baptist was the herald of good news (1:2-3). What did he say and do to get things ready for Jesus' arrival (1:4-8)?

John's hearers were steeped in the story of the exodus from Egypt when God dramatically brought Israel through the Red Sea (Exodus 14). What connections might John want them to make with this story as he invited them to be baptised in the Jordan River?

3. What did Jesus see and hear as he emerged from the waters of his baptism (1:9-11)?

Read Isaiah 42:1 (introducing the suffering servant), Psalm 2:7 (God greeting the messianic king as his Son) and Genesis 22:2 (God's command to Abraham regarding his son). Considering these, what impact might his Father's words have had on Jesus?

4. What did the Spirit do and what happened in the desert (1:12-13)?

How does this help us understand the battle Jesus was drawn into?

5. Mark 1:15 sums up Jesus' message. What do you understand it to mean?

John's baptism

In the Old Testament, God brought his people out of Egypt and led them into the wilderness. They had much to learn about being his people. So, John's call to come out into the desert and to repent would have resonated with people as a call to renew relationship with God. Israel must come again into the wilderness, acknowledging disobedience, in preparation for a new covenant with God. But John's baptism was novel. At the time, handwashing and immersion in water were practised by pious Jews to cleanse themselves from impurity. But they were self-administered. In contrast, it is John who immerses people in the river in preparation for the coming of God.

Going Deeper ○

6. Read Isaiah 9:1-7; 40:1-5; 53:1-12; and 61:1-7. In what ways do these prophecies shed light on the gospel (1:1), 'the good news of God' (1:14), the fulfilment of Israel's hope and God's promised salvation?

7. Read the feature article on the kingdom of God on page 28. How is this announcement of God's kingship revolutionary and joyful?

Living it Out (((o)))

8. How does Mark's introduction to Jesus, his identity, and his purpose in this passage help you be confident and courageous in your everyday life under God?

9. What, if anything, seems a battle on your frontline?

How might Jesus' announcement of the in-breaking kingdom of God shape your response to this battle?

10. We repent and believe when we become Christians and continue to do so throughout our discipleship. How might you need to repent and believe today?

Responding in Prayer

- Thank God together for what you've seen of Jesus in this passage and what he came to do.

- In twos or threes, pray through one another's responses to questions 9 and 10.

- Ask God to bring to mind someone you'd love to draw closer to Jesus. In pairs, pray for these people, drawing on the insights of your discussion to shape your prayers.

Mark and the Old Testament

Mark draws extensively on the Old Testament, particularly the prophet Isaiah, to explain what God is doing. As well as specific references, he alludes to the Old Testament in other ways. For example, Mark uses the same word for 'beginning' in 1:1 that's used in Genesis 1:1 and so stirs his hearers into a state of heightened anticipation. The God who brought order out of chaos at creation was now doing the 'new thing' that Isaiah had foretold (Isaiah 43:19). Another example is the way that Mark alludes to the Israelite exodus from Egypt. Mark is helping his hearers understand that this is the exodus story happening over again. This time God is setting his people free once and for all. The quote in verses 2–3 combines Exodus 23:20, Malachi 3:1, and Isaiah 40:3 but is ascribed to Isaiah. This isn't a mistake. Mark is placing the story of John the Baptist and Jesus in the context of Isaiah's vision that, one day, God would act decisively to restore and renew Israel, and the whole world.

Jesus and the kingdom of God

The good news of Jesus can be summed up in the announcement that the kingdom of God has come (1:14-15). From the beginning it's clear that the 'kingdom of God' is key to understanding Jesus and his mission.

Interestingly, Mark never abbreviates to 'kingdom', always using the full phrase, 'the kingdom of God'. He uses the phrase relatively infrequently (fourteen times) in his Gospel. But the emphasis is on God reigning. It describes a relationship that people enter with God himself – God is their king. It also describes regime change – God has taken control of the world in a new way.

For Mark, the Old Testament told a kingdom story. Mark's account of the kingdom of God is rooted in God's dealings with Israel. His frequent allusions to the Old Testament help his hearers grasp the significance of Jesus' revolutionary announcement. When seen in the flow of God's work in the world through the generations, what Jesus proclaims and demonstrates is truly joyous news.

God is the creator, and Israel God's chosen people, a light to the nations. They were to be witnesses to his goodness and love and demonstrate what living faithfully and fruitfully under his kingship looked like, a blessing to the world. It didn't work out. Though there were some bright moments in their story, in the end they failed. By the time Jesus burst onto the scene, the lived experience of the Jews was that of prolonged exile. They keenly felt God's absence. They prayed for the restoration of Israel and God's kingly rule in their lifetime. They lived in hope.

The good news that Mark heralded in his Gospel was that their longed-for Messiah had come. Their hopes were being realised, but not as they had expected. Through his life, teaching, death, and resurrection, King Jesus confounded people. His parables (Mark 4) describing the kingdom of God gave notice that his reign didn't operate along human lines. Money, power, politics – all were upended. No wonder it was a kingship that many rejected. For this was an upside-down kingdom – the first would be last and the last first. What's more, the kingdom would grow in ways they could not foresee or control, and beyond the Jews alone. Power dynamics would be revolutionised, most profoundly through Jesus' suffering, service, and sacrificial love. It was a model of kingship neither the disciples nor the Jewish leaders anticipated.

So, has the kingdom of God come? Is the kingdom of God still to come? Yes to both. Mark's Gospel reveals that the kingdom of God decisively broke into our world through the work of God in Christ. One day, though, it will come in all its fullness, when Jesus returns. This 'now, not yet' tension is sometimes illustrated using the Allies' victory in World War II. On D-Day, 6 June 1944, for all practical purposes the war in Europe was won when the Allies successfully invaded northern France. But it wasn't until 8 May 1945, Victory in Europe (VE) Day, that the war was finally over.

It's clear from Jesus' parables about the kingdom of God that we can wait for and welcome it (4:26-29; 4:30-32). Elsewhere in his Gospel, Mark affirms that we can know the secrets of the kingdom of God, we can enter it, and be close to it (4:11; 9:47; 10:23-25; 12:34). But there's no suggestion that we can build it or hasten its coming. Mark makes it very clear that the kingdom of God is God's revolution. But as we walk with Jesus our King, we learn to live in the kingdom of God, offering glimpses to the world of the fullness of life in Christ in all its new-creation wonder. Only his resurrection power can fuel it (Ephesians 1:15-23).

Session 2

Demonstrating Authority

Mark 4:35–41

First Thoughts

The remains of an ancient Galilean boat, dating from the first century AD and discovered during a drought in 1986, are currently displayed at the Yigal Allon Museum on the shore of the Sea of Galilee. Sometimes called the 'Jesus Boat', it's a beautifully preserved example of the kind of boat used in Jesus' day.

The Sea or Lake of Galilee is known by different names in the Bible – Tiberias (John 6:1), Gennesaret (Luke 5:1), Kinnereth (Numbers 34:11). The River Jordan flows through the lake, which is about 13 miles long and 8 miles wide. Remarkably, it's the lowest freshwater lake on our planet.

Its low-lying position together with the high, almost unbroken wall of hills around it meant the lake was subject to sudden, violent storms. The Sea of Galilee is relatively shallow and so its waters would be rapidly whipped up by the wind, posing an immediate danger to small boats caught out on the lake.

At the time of Jesus, there was a thriving fishing industry around the lake with lots of trade and ferrying by boat. As another bustling day around and on the lake drew to a close, Jesus emerged from an exhausting time of teaching with the crowd unwilling to disperse. As evening closed in, he decided they would ferry themselves over to the other side of the lake. In one sense, it was such an ordinary day. But ordinary days become extraordinary when the King of kings and Lord of all is amongst us.

Read – Mark 4:35-41

35 That day when evening came, he said to his disciples, 'Let us go over to the other side.' 36 Leaving the crowd behind, they took him along, just as he was, in the boat. There were also other boats with him. 37 A furious squall came up, and the waves broke over the boat, so that it was nearly swamped. 38 Jesus was in the stern, sleeping on a cushion. The disciples woke him and said to him, 'Teacher, don't you care if we drown?'

39 He got up, rebuked the wind and said to the waves, 'Quiet! Be still!' Then the wind died down and it was completely calm.

40 He said to his disciples, 'Why are you so afraid? Do you still have no faith?'

41 They were terrified and asked each other, 'Who is this? Even the wind and the waves obey him!'

Focus on the Theme

1. Who's your hero? Think about someone (other than Jesus) who has been a positive and influential figure in your life. What difference did they make and why?

What Does the Bible Say?

2. What strikes you about Jesus' behaviour in this account (4:35-39)?

3. How would you describe the disciples' emotional state before and after Jesus calms the storm (4:38, 40-41)?

How would you explain the change?

4. Read Job 38:8-11 and Psalm 107:23-32. What light do these Old Testament passages shed on the story of Jesus calming the storm?

5. Another way of expressing Jesus' question in 4:40 is: 'Where is your faith?' What did the disciples need to learn about Jesus, the object of their faith?

Going Deeper

6. Mark 4:35-41 is the first in a series of miracles that Mark reports in quick succession. Read on through 5:1-43. How does Mark use these miracles to demonstrate the scope of Jesus' power and authority?

7. Read the account of Jonah (Jonah 1-2). What parallels do you see in Mark 4:35-41?

How is Jesus 'greater than Jonah' (Matthew 12:40-41)?

Living it Out

Responding in Prayer

8. In twos or threes, share any storms you're in. To what extent are you able to trust Jesus' authority in these?

9. How does this passage shape your daily dependence on God on your frontlines?

10. On the cross, Jesus was victorious against the ultimate storm of sin and death. How does knowing this help you turn to him when you go through tough experiences that perhaps you don't understand?

- Pray, asking God how he wants to be Lord of your storms and to bring you peace.

- 'Help me believe.' Pray this for one another in the light of what you want to trust him for.

- Ask God to bring to mind someone you'd love to draw closer to Jesus. In pairs, pray for these people, drawing on the insights of your discussion to shape your prayers.

Miracles and mighty deeds

In subduing the sea and wind, Jesus demonstrated his power to the disciples and revealed himself as God's saving and sovereign presence amongst them. The forces of nature submit to him, just as they did to the God of Israel when the Israelites crossed the Red Sea in the exodus from Egypt. Only God can do this.

This passage is the first of three miracles – the Greek word *dynameis* means 'deeds of power' – that Mark reports in quick succession. But there are many others in the Gospel – healings, feeding miracles, exorcisms, raising from the dead. It's interesting to note, too, Jesus' reluctance to perform miracles at times, the paucity of miracles in his hometown, and Jesus' exhortation sometimes to keep quiet about what people had seen or experienced.

So, what are we to make of the miracles, the deeds of power that Jesus performs throughout the Gospel? How should we understand Jesus' refusal to grant the Pharisees' request for a sign?

Jesus' miracles point to his identity and vocation. They were deeds of power connected with his proclamation that 'the kingdom of God has come'. In other words, they signposted the astonishing truth that God's healing, restoring future had broken into the present, and this is what it looks like with God in charge. Jesus didn't claim to be a miracle-worker. Rather, he was God amongst them, and this reality was powerfully implicit through his mighty deeds. His, then, was a power that could face up to evil and cosmic conflict and overcome. His was an authority that could forgive sins, and he signals his power to do so.

Mark never connects 'signs' (Greek word *sēmeia*) positively with Jesus' ministry (8:11-12; 13:22). Jesus despaired at the Pharisees' demand for a sign from heaven to authenticate his identity and authority. He would not perform a miracle only to persuade the unbelieving. Jesus performed few miracles in Nazareth (6:1-6) and this might suggest a link between believing in Jesus and the work he does. However, Jesus' power to heal isn't dependent on belief. Rather, it's wrapped up into establishing his identity and proclaiming the good news of the kingdom.

GARETH'S STORY

During the Covid pandemic, work changed radically for Gareth and his team, as for so many. Ordinarily, the 360-acre farm they worked from was home to a host of programmes supporting young people and their families in crisis. So, when they had to shut these down, Gareth and his team asked God what he wanted them to do with the facilities, gifts, and resources they had. The answer was 'food'.

Wonderfully, they were able to pivot and turn their resources into a distribution centre for food boxes which would then be delivered to local families in crisis. 'We've been awed at the way God has worked, not only providing for families through us, but opening up conversations on doorsteps and creating opportunities for us to pray for people who often tell us such heart-rending stories,' Gareth shared. God had faithfully continued to lead them in his ways as messengers of a hope-filled gospel.

Wrapped up into this has been running the distribution centre. That's been challenging and faith-stretching too. But, as Gareth commented, 'I've noticed just how many stories of God's provision we now have to tell.' About tomatoes, for example.

Tomatoes weren't the only fruit God provided

The team needed a lot of tomatoes for their food boxes and, one time, the tomatoes just didn't turn up. A few of the team gathered to pray. Shortly afterwards, someone rang Gareth to say they had some fruit and vegetables that might be helpful for the project. 'What have you got?' Gareth asked. 'Tomatoes,' he replied. 'No way! How many have you got?' Gareth asked, imagining a couple of punnets. '25 kilos, and we can get them to you within the hour.' The team needed 20 kilos. By the time they had to start packing the boxes, the tomatoes had arrived, and every box went out full.

This is just one of many experiences Gareth and his team have had of God's generous provision. Their faith has grown. 'If God can supply tomatoes, then we can trust him for the people and finances we need,' Gareth said. It's started to change the way they pray. One time, they needed a certain kind of van. They asked themselves: 'Do we believe that God can provide us with such a van?' 'Yes,' they agreed. Their prayer shifted: '*How*, Lord, would you like to provide us with the van we need?' Well, that's another story; another story of God's mighty deeds, his unexpected ways, and his loving faithfulness in drawing his people into his wondrous work in the world.

Session 3

Revealing Identity

Mark 8:27–38

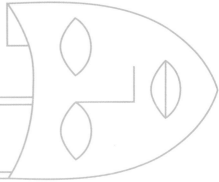

First Thoughts

We've arrived at the turning point of the book. In the second half, Mark will increasingly direct our attention towards what Jesus came to do. But up to this point, Mark has focused on giving us eyes to see who Jesus is, and it climaxes here in Peter's confession: 'You are the Messiah.'

Contemporary Western society wrestles with identity. Identity politics, online personas, 'finding your true self' have become commonplace phrases and sometimes cause conflict and confusion. Marketing campaigns capitalise on the anxieties of our times, creating idealised identities in relation to our sense of who we are and what we're worth.

Identity really matters. It's a central theme in the Bible. Our sense of identity profoundly impacts our capacity to flourish. But in tackling the questions about who we truly are, the Bible starts from a different place and with a different question: who is God? For it's the answer to this question that unlocks our identity and our humanity: who we are in relation to God himself.

By chapter 8, Jesus' disciples have lived around Jesus for some while. They've been mesmerised by his teaching and perplexed by his parables. They've witnessed his authority over nature, sickness, and demons, and heard his wisdom with the crowds. They've observed how he upended convention and challenged convictions, and they've seen the difference his compassion and his power make. Of course, they won't get their heads around the events Jesus predicts for a while longer. But they've come to believe this: Jesus is the Christ, their hoped-for Messiah, God's anointed one.

Read – Mark 8:27-38

²⁷ Jesus and his disciples went on to the villages around Caesarea Philippi. On the way he asked them, 'Who do people say I am?'

²⁸ They replied, 'Some say John the Baptist; others say Elijah; and still others, one of the prophets.'

²⁹ 'But what about you?' he asked. 'Who do you say I am?'

Peter answered, 'You are the Messiah.'

³⁰ Jesus warned them not to tell anyone about him.

³¹ He then began to teach them that the Son of Man must suffer many things and be rejected by the elders, the chief priests and the teachers of the law, and that he must be killed and after three days rise again. ³² He spoke plainly about this, and Peter took him aside and began to rebuke him.

[33] But when Jesus turned and looked at his disciples, he rebuked Peter. 'Get behind me, Satan!' he said. 'You do not have in mind the concerns of God, but merely human concerns.'

[34] Then he called the crowd to him along with his disciples and said: 'Whoever wants to be my disciple must deny themselves and take up their cross and follow me. [35] For whoever wants to save their life will lose it, but whoever loses their life for me and for the gospel will save it. [36] What good is it for someone to gain the whole world, yet forfeit their soul? [37] Or what can anyone give in exchange for their soul? [38] If anyone is ashamed of me and my words in this adulterous and sinful generation, the Son of Man will be ashamed of them when he comes in his Father's glory with the holy angels.'

Elijah and John the Baptist

People were right to describe Jesus as one of Israel's prophets. But he certainly wasn't John the Baptist brought back to life, nor Elijah, as people speculated (6:14-15; 8:28). In fact, it is John the Baptist whom Jesus identifies as the Elijah who is to come (Matthew 11:14). This was to fulfil Malachi's prophecy that a messenger would come to prepare the way of the Lord (Malachi 3:1; 4:5-6; Mark 1:2-3). Notice how Mark's description of John (1:6) is close to that of Elijah in 2 Kings 1:8.

Focus on the Theme

1. Think about a time when you discovered something about a friend, family member, or colleague that helped you understand them more deeply. Briefly describe this to one another and how that shaped your relationship with them.

What Does the Bible Say?

2. When Peter answered Jesus' question about his identity in 8:29, what had he grasped?

Why might Jesus have commanded the disciples to keep quiet about his identity (8:30)?

3. When Jesus connected suffering with the long hoped-for Messiah (8:31) this made no sense to the disciples. Why do you think Peter reacted in the way he did (8:32)?

4. What does Jesus teach about the cost of discipleship (8:34-35)?

5. Mark 8:38 echoes the vision of Daniel 7:13-14 and its description of a heavenly enthronement. Jesus, the Son of Man, is destined to be enthroned as judge and king over all. In what ways does this add weight to Jesus' call to follow him?

Son of Man

6. 'Son of Man' is how Mark most commonly identifies Jesus in his Gospel. Divide these passages amongst the group to read aloud: 2:9–11, 23–28; 8:31; 10:41–45; 13:26–27; 14:60–62. How does Mark answer the question, 'Who is this Son of Man?'

7. In 8:31; 9:31; and 10:32–34, Jesus warns the disciples about what is going to happen to him. His vocation echoes Isaiah's prophecy about the suffering servant (Isaiah 52:13–53:12). How does the pattern set by Jesus shape our attitude to suffering in our own discipleship?

In referring to himself, Jesus used the title 'Son of Man' far more than any other. We find it eighty-two times across the four Gospels, most frequently in Matthew. It occurs fourteen times in Mark. The phrase simply means 'human being'. But the title has prophetic overtones. It's how God refers to Ezekiel throughout his prophetic ministry. In Mark's Gospel it variously points to Jesus' authority, his suffering, his vindication, and his power. Daniel 7 provides the clue to a deeper meaning. The context in Daniel is the same as that in Mark — opposition, suffering, and vindication. Daniel's vision is of 'one like a son of man' who is given dominion, glory, and kingship. Applying the term to himself as a representative of humanity, Jesus affirms that he is the bearer of God's plan to overthrow evil and be the way to the fullness of God's reign. As in Daniel's vision, it would require intense suffering.

Living it Out

8. Jesus rebuked Peter for thinking as a mere mortal and not from God's perspective (8:33). Imagine you're talking with Jesus about one of your frontlines. What assumptions, if any, might Jesus want to overturn?

9. Lifelong discipleship is rooted in an open and unreserved commitment to Jesus and his ways in the world. What, then, might it look like for you to 'take up your cross' and follow Jesus in your everyday life right now?

10. In today's world, identity is often linked to performance or achievement. Jesus' radical challenge to lose the old self and take on a new identity is founded in the lavish love of God. How might this be liberating for you?

Responding in Prayer

- Take a few moments of silent personal prayer to share with God your thoughts and feelings from the study. At the end, pray Samuel's prayer to the Lord (1 Samuel 3:10): 'Speak, for your servant is listening.' Hold a moment of silence.

- As a group, use some short prayers to express to God something of what struck you about Jesus from your discussion or something from your silent prayer time.

- Ask God to bring to mind someone you'd love to draw closer to Jesus. In pairs, pray for these people, drawing on the insights of your discussion to shape your prayers.

The Messiah, the Christ

Those who were longing for a messiah were hoping for God's chosen one who would bring in God's kingdom, restoring Israel's independence and righteousness. They expected their messiah to do three things: rebuild, or cleanse, the temple, defeat the enemy of God's people, and bring in God's justice. Their hopes for a messiah became tied to other aspirations such as freedom from Gentile, especially Roman, domination.

But Jesus confounded their expectations. He didn't gather a military army. His suffering and death had no precedent in Jewish hopes of a messiah. Jesus redefined their notion of messiahship.

The Greek word for messiah is *christos* and comes from the verb 'to anoint'. It refers to the practice of anointing someone with oil when they're installed in a special office such as king or priest. Jesus is the Anointed One. His was a new way of being God's anointed king.

Making sense of Jesus' parables

Jesus' teaching style memorably includes the use of parables. The term comes from the Greek *parabolē* meaning comparison. So, parables are stories or sayings that illustrate a truth by using some form of analogy. Their meaning isn't always easy to grasp so they can sometimes read more like riddles, particularly if we don't spot some of the code that can be embedded in the stories.

It seems that Jesus' disciples struggled to understand them. In chapter 4 of Mark's Gospel, Jesus uses several parables to teach about the kingdom of God: the sower and the seed, the lamp on a stand, the growing seed, the mustard seed. He draws on familiar, everyday contexts – homes, fields, nature – and invites people to a fresh understanding of how God works. It's not always through powerful pyrotechnics as with Moses on Mount Sinai (Exodus 19:16–19) or direct interventions such as Jesus' baptism (Mark 1:10–11), though God can and does work that way. But God also works slowly, subtly, in ways that resonate with rhythms of seasons and agricultural cycles. It's perhaps not surprising that the disciples and

others struggled to make sense of these parables as descriptions of the kingdom of God. They were expecting a lot more drama with a radical regime change.

Parables can also be pregnant with meaning through allusion to other parts of God's story. In a sense, the parable of the sower (4:1-20) sets up much of what will unfold through the rest of the Gospel. God is sowing in the land again after years of exile. Some seed will flourish and some fail. Misunderstanding and resistance will arise as well as plentiful harvests.

People have puzzled over Mark 4:9-12. Is Jesus deliberately limiting the possibility of people coming to faith by using parables with 'outsiders' to keep people from understanding? It doesn't seem to fit with what we know of Jesus in the Bible. Nor does it fit with what we see of the disciples in Mark's Gospel. These 'insiders' who are supposed to 'get it' just don't. Indeed, there's an ironic comparison between some 'outsiders' who demonstrate faith and understanding — the Syrophoenician woman (7:24-30); the Roman centurion who witnessed Jesus' death (15:39) - and the disciples, 'insiders' who seem perpetually confused (8:14–21).

Jesus does seem to be saying something about people's ability to miss what's under their nose; to see, yet not understand; to not realise even what they don't know. He's on a mission, announcing the arrival of the kingdom of God. Not everyone will respond. He also has the challenge of reframing people's understanding of what this looks like, of renewing their minds and winning their hearts. Hence, the need for secrecy. A reputation as a miracle worker, for example, would obscure the heart of Jesus' revelation of who he is and what he's there to do.

The conquering power of King Jesus is exercised through service and suffering and sacrifice, ultimately through his cross and resurrection. And if this is the way of King Jesus then this must be reflected in the kingdom of God. The parables in Mark's Gospel seem to be one way that Jesus provokes people to 'repent and believe'; to turn around and go in a completely new and unexpected direction, putting their trust wholly in him.

Session 4

Challenging Allegiance

Mark 10:17–31

First Thoughts

God rules all things through King Jesus. This was the contested truth that Jesus announced and enacted. There could be no greater declaration of power and authority. What's more, he demanded a response. Come follow me.

There's no way round it. We're called to bow the knee before the King, to pledge allegiance to him above all others and above all things. In our society, inclined to be suspicious of power, this goes completely against the grain. How often we've seen power misused and abused; voices silenced or sidelined. Power tends to corrupt, and absolute power corrupts absolutely, declared Lord Acton in 1887. We tend to agree. Some of us bear the scars.

Jesus is on his way to Jerusalem. In a few short chapters, he will be nailed to the cross, a crown of thorns on his head, mocked as 'king of the Jews'. When Joseph takes Jesus' body down from the cross and wraps it in burial linen, he will see the wounds, and probably weep.

Jesus is King like no other. We pledge allegiance to him,

'Who, being in very nature God,
Did not consider equality with God something to be grasped,
But made himself nothing,
Taking the very nature of a servant,
being made in human likeness.
And being found in appearance as a man,
he humbled himself
and became obedient to death—
even death on a cross!'
Philippians 2:6–8

Read – Mark 10:17-31

¹⁷ As Jesus started on his way, a man ran up to him and fell on his knees before him. 'Good teacher,' he asked, 'what must I do to inherit eternal life?'

¹⁸ 'Why do you call me good?' Jesus answered. 'No one is good—except God alone. ¹⁹ You know the commandments: "You shall not murder, you shall not commit adultery, you shall not steal, you shall not give false testimony, you shall not defraud, honour your father and mother."'

²⁰ 'Teacher,' he declared, 'all these I have kept since I was a boy.'

²¹ Jesus looked at him and loved him. 'One thing you lack,' he said. 'Go, sell everything you have and give to the poor, and you will have treasure in heaven. Then come, follow me.'

²² At this the man's face fell. He went away sad, because he had great wealth.

²³ Jesus looked round and said to his disciples, 'How hard it is for the rich to enter the kingdom of God!'

²⁴ The disciples were amazed at his words. But Jesus said again, 'Children, how hard it is to enter the kingdom of God! ²⁵ It is easier for a camel to go through the eye of a needle than for someone who is rich to enter the kingdom of God.'

²⁶ The disciples were even more amazed, and said to each other, 'Who then can be saved?'

²⁷ Jesus looked at them and said, 'With man this is impossible, but not with God; all things are possible with God.'

²⁸ Then Peter spoke up, 'We have left everything to follow you!'

²⁹ 'Truly I tell you,' Jesus replied, 'no one who has left home or brothers or sisters or mother or father or children or fields for me and the gospel ³⁰ will fail to receive a hundred times as much in this present age: homes, brothers, sisters, mothers, children and fields—along with persecutions—and in the age to come eternal life. ³¹ But many who are first will be last, and the last first.'

Focus on the Theme ⊕

What Does the Bible Say? 🔖

1. In what area of your life, if any, do you have a sense of power or being in control? Briefly describe what this is like, how you tend to feel and act.

2. Considering what the rich man likely understood by 'eternal life' (see box), how would you express his question (10:17) in your own words?

3. Read Exodus 20:1-17. What do you notice about the commandments Jesus refers to in his answer (10:19) and those he omits?

How does Jesus' response in 10:21 relate to the commandments around idolatry and covetousness?

4. In your own words, what does Jesus say in 10:23-25?

What do you make of the disciples' reaction (10:26) and Jesus' response (10:27)?

5. What gains does Jesus describe for his disciples now and in the age to come (10:29-31)?

Going Deeper 🔍

6. In what ways do Mark 9:33–37 and 12:28–34 resonate with this passage?

7. Two healings of blind men (Mark 8:22–26 and 10:46–52) act like bookends around Jesus' teaching on discipleship as he journeys to Jerusalem. Read 8:22–10:52. What strikes you afresh?

Eternal life — the age to come

First-century Jews were accustomed to thinking about the 'present age' and the 'age to come'. The 'present age', which they were living in, was marked by oppression, sin, and injustice. The 'age to come' they expected to be ushered in by a great event bringing freedom, peace, justice, and judgment. God would renew the whole world and the righteous would be raised to new life, Jews generally believed. The 'kingdom of God' is another way of expressing this hope. Naturally, many Jews wanted to be sure they would be part of this. Leading Jews would have answered the rich man's question with an interpretation of the law. Jesus' response required a radical rethink about what it meant to put God first.

Living it Out ((o))

8. How would you describe your own attitude towards money?

In what ways, if any, does your frontline shape your attitude towards money?

9. For you, what would be the main warning sign that your allegiance to Jesus is divided?

What might you do to protect yourself against the love of money, or other idols?

10. Jesus is the true rich, young man (in some translations 'ruler'). Yet, for our sakes, he became poor (2 Corinthians 8:9). How might Jesus' love-driven sacrifice help you to trust him with all that you have and are?

Responding in Prayer

- Use the ACTS framework to shape your prayers from your discussion, particularly focusing on ways in which you steward your money or other resources:

  - Adore – Give God praise that Jesus is Lord of all

  - Confess – Tell him what you're sorry for and seek his power to change

  - Thanksgiving – Tell him what you're grateful for

  - Supplication – Ask for God's help to handle your money as Jesus' disciple

- Ask God to bring to mind someone you'd love to draw closer to Jesus. In pairs, pray for these people, drawing on the insights of your discussion to shape your prayers.

The eye of the needle

All kinds of theories have been offered to explain this phrase. One popular explanation was that, in Jesus' day, there was a narrow gate in Jerusalem's walls called 'The Eye of the Needle' which opened after the main gate was closed at night. A camel could not pass through it unless its baggage was removed. There's no evidence such a gate existed. In fact, Jesus here is deliberately exaggerating to vividly make his point: someone's riches can no more guarantee them a place in the kingdom of God than a camel can pass through the eye of a needle. Instead, there would be treasure stored up in heaven, in the 'age to come'. This would have challenged first-century Jews' perspective on wealth which was usually seen as reward for living a good life.

Discipleship in Mark

The disciples don't often shine in Mark's Gospel. They begin well – leaving everything to follow Jesus – and they have some good moments when out on mission (Mark 6). Largely, though, they fail to understand Jesus, grow more confused, display some poor judgment, and finally abandon him, one having betrayed him and at least one other denying him.

It's likely Mark intended the early Christian communities to identify with the disciples. Committed to Jesus, there was nevertheless so much they still had to learn about living his way in their world. Likewise, for us today. The gospel invites us to do life with Jesus, always. Therein lies the mystery, the secret. If it's life with Jesus, it's life with one who is both suffering servant and victorious king.

A disciple is a learner, and Mark was eager for his hearers to grasp what it meant to respond to Jesus as his disciples or apprentices. In Jesus' day, rabbis didn't invite disciples to follow them. Rather, those who wanted to learn would choose a rabbi they thought would best instruct them in the law. So, it was quickly clear to the disciples that Jesus was forging a new path by calling them to himself. He chose them to be with him and not because they possessed outstanding qualities or devotion. Nor because they were showing promise in religious circles. Jesus called them in the midst of their daily work.

They were clearly very much a work-in-progress. Just as the blind man's sight was restored first in part (8:22-26), their 'sight' remains blurred, their incomprehension evident throughout Mark's Gospel. But Jesus is unfailingly committed to them and later they will see clearly. Jesus will come into focus for the disciples when they experience his risen presence and start to grasp the wonder of his kingdom good news. But that's another story.

Mark presents the bulk of Jesus' teaching on discipleship on the journey to Jerusalem (8:22-10:52) and, as in the other Gospels, the requirements are radically demanding. The content varies, though. Mark doesn't record Jesus teaching the 'Lord's Prayer', for example.

Yet there's something to learn from the way that Mark tells the story of Jesus. From the disciples' perspective, it's a story of unexpected twists and turns, one of gradual revelation. The way that we grow as disciples can be a bit like that, too. Discipleship isn't a programme we enrol in. It's a life we immerse ourselves in – the life of Jesus. And that can be confusing and demanding, as well as exhilarating, and more. For he's good, but not safe, as Mr Beaver described Aslan in *The Lion, the Witch and the Wardrobe*. He's the King.

Mark's Gospel is primarily the story of Jesus who came on the scene announcing a dramatic new move of God – the kingdom of God has come. It's the account of Jesus, Son of God, who embraced an unimaginable death out of love, and was then raised to life, victorious over death.

The cross shapes Jesus' identity and his way in the world as King. It's the central image of discipleship in Mark. Jesus is clear: to follow him is to imitate his pattern of sacrificial love, to be willing to suffer, shamefully if needed, and to stick with him (8:34). It's an uncompromising call to put God first. And trust.

For God is faithful. Mark's distinctive account of the good news of Jesus makes it clear that it's the culmination of a story of God's dealing with his people over generations. So, discipleship isn't only learning the way of Jesus in our contexts in our times. It's grasping how God's plans for all time and eternity find their fulfilment in Jesus.

LEXI'S STORY

The whispering, combined with Anna's not-so-subtle glances in Lexi's direction made it obvious she was talking about her. It was ridiculous; two months had passed, but Anna still bore a grudge. Eyes fixed on her keyboard, Lexi battled the urge to stride over to Anna's desk and tell her exactly how petty she was being. Gradually, the red mist evaporated, and that familiar, heavy feeling of just wanting to get out of there resumed.

A few months earlier, a rare opportunity for promotion had arisen within the team. Anna and Lexi both applied. Lexi got the nod. Until that moment, they'd been quite close. Anna was a complex and private woman, but their mutual love of running had provided plenty of opportunity to chat. Resultingly, a level of warmth and trust had grown.

But that was then, and this was now. It was a painful season for Lexi. Her cheerful (and then hopeful) 'Good morning' greetings would go unreturned. And she dreaded the semi-frequent moments she'd have to approach Anna's desk to ask her something work-related, where, at best, she'd receive a curt reply.

Lexi prayed a lot in this time. She knew she needed to. She was aware of her fight or flight response kicking in regularly, and she didn't want this to dictate her behaviour. She was committed to living the way of Jesus in her little patch of his world.

Waiting for the thaw

So, amidst the tension and distress, Lexi practised patience. She asked God for endurance and wisdom, and enrolled prayer support from her good friend and her small group. She prayed for Anna and asked God to show her how to talk and act in a way that might demonstrate to Anna that she cared for her.

After a few months, Anna's iciness began to thaw. The 'Good morning' greetings were returned, and Anna's responses became less brusque. Small talk crept back in, even laughter.

Some months later, another position was created, and this time Anna was successful. Now, they work well together, one helping the other when they can see they are struggling. They have fun and, if anything, the relationship is deeper now than it was before. Sometimes Anna seeks out Lexi's advice, even sharing quite personal things. In those moments, Lexi pinches herself, because she remembers how things were. And she's thankful. She'd experienced God's transforming power in her own life just as much as she'd seen him work in Anna's.

Session 5

Transforming Power

Mark 14:32–52

First Thoughts

They really were unprepared for it, those disciples. They didn't have a clue. And who could blame them. This was so new, so unexpected, so... crazy. Jesus just didn't conform.

He didn't conform to who they expected their king to be. He didn't conform to what they'd expected their messiah to do. He seemed to be on a path that made no sense of God's promise to return to rescue and restore them, to dwell amongst them once more. Jesus' words to the disciples in the garden of Gethsemane were clouded by their incomprehension, not just their sleepiness. They certainly longed for God's kingdom. But they never expected the cross.

Yet God was on the move. The mysterious strands of his saving plan revealed through the centuries were coming together in Jesus – royal figure, suffering servant, Son of Man, Messiah, God's Holy One.

So, what was the true nature of God's power? What was God doing about evil? Where was his saving, healing, restorative justice? How would God's kingdom come?

In answer, Mark points us to the 'cup' and then on to the cross. The full forces of evil, the weight of sin at every level, and the destructive power of death would do their worst in the most violent battle of all time. Jesus would be at its centre, alone. It would be agony in every way.

And Jesus said, 'Yes'.

Read – Mark 14:32–52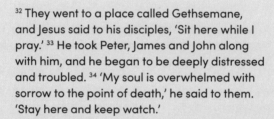

[32] They went to a place called Gethsemane, and Jesus said to his disciples, 'Sit here while I pray.' [33] He took Peter, James and John along with him, and he began to be deeply distressed and troubled. [34] 'My soul is overwhelmed with sorrow to the point of death,' he said to them. 'Stay here and keep watch.'

[35] Going a little farther, he fell to the ground and prayed that if possible the hour might pass from him. [36] 'Abba, Father,' he said, 'everything is possible for you. Take this cup from me. Yet not what I will, but what you will.'

[37] Then he returned to his disciples and found them sleeping. 'Simon,' he said to Peter, 'are you asleep? Couldn't you keep watch for one hour? [38] Watch and pray so that you will not fall into temptation. The spirit is willing, but the flesh is weak.'

[39] Once more he went away and prayed the same thing. [40] When he came back, he again found them sleeping, because their eyes were heavy. They did not know what to say to him.

[41] Returning the third time, he said to them, 'Are you still sleeping and resting? Enough! The hour has come. Look, the Son of Man is delivered into the hands of sinners. [42] Rise! Let us go! Here comes my betrayer!'

⁴³ Just as he was speaking, Judas, one of the Twelve, appeared. With him was a crowd armed with swords and clubs, sent from the chief priests, the teachers of the law, and the elders.

⁴⁴ Now the betrayer had arranged a signal with them: 'The one I kiss is the man; arrest him and lead him away under guard.' ⁴⁵ Going at once to Jesus, Judas said, 'Rabbi!' and kissed him. ⁴⁶ The men seized Jesus and arrested him. ⁴⁷ Then one of those standing near drew his sword and struck the servant of the high priest, cutting off his ear.

⁴⁸ 'Am I leading a rebellion,' said Jesus, 'that you have come out with swords and clubs to capture me? ⁴⁹ Every day I was with you, teaching in the temple courts, and you did not arrest me. But the Scriptures must be fulfilled.' ⁵⁰ Then everyone deserted him and fled.

⁵¹ A young man, wearing nothing but a linen garment, was following Jesus. When they seized him, ⁵² he fled naked, leaving his garment behind.

Gethsemane

'Gethsemane' gets its name from the Aramaic word for oil press. It lay east of Jerusalem across the Kidron Valley on the Mount of Olives. Considered to be within Jerusalem, the olive grove was an acceptable place for Passover pilgrims to stay for Passover night. John's Gospel describes it as a garden, suggesting it may have been a walled enclosure.

Focus on the Theme

1. Have you ever witnessed someone who is usually strong and in control start to fall apart?

What was the effect on you?

What Does the Bible Say? 🔖

2. Consider Jesus' distress in 14:32–36. What is the 'cup' that provokes such anguish?

Why is this so deeply troubling for Jesus?

What's your response to seeing Jesus' distress?

3. How does Jesus come through this great struggle (14:36)?

How does this connect with his teaching in 9:23; 10:27; and 11:24?

4. Jesus declares 'the hour has come' (14:41). The drama announced in 1:15, which is the arrival of the reign of God, is to be fulfilled. How does Hebrews 5:7–8 shed light on Jesus' willingness to align with God's will and to suffer?

5. In what ways does Jesus' arrest signal that the kingdom of God is totally different from the kingdom of the world (14:43–50)?

The cup

In the Old Testament, the prophets refer to 'the cup' as a metaphor for God's wrath and judgment (Ezekiel 23:32–34; Isaiah 51:17–23; Jeremiah 25:15). God's justice is poured out onto injustice, dealing with humanity's sin and its effects. Now, through Jesus' suffering love and victorious confrontation with evil at every level, death, the final enemy, would be defeated; people would be set free, and creation renewed.

Going Deeper

6. Recall another garden scene where people were tested – the Garden of Eden in the book of Genesis (Genesis 2:15-16; 3:1-7). What is the same and what is different about what happens in the Garden of Gethsemane?

How does looking at Gethsemane as an echo of Eden help us gain a richer understanding of what was going on here?

7. Read Deuteronomy 21:22-23; 2 Corinthians 5:21; Galatians 3:13-14. Meditate on Jesus' cry in Mark 15:34 and the tearing of the temple curtain in 15:38. How are God's love and justice both powerful and transforming?

Living it Out

8. In what ways do you identify with the disciples in the garden?

The disciples failed to follow Jesus' instructions and didn't spot the significance of the unfolding events. How is your grasp of God's grace deepened as you consider Jesus going on alone to the cross?

9. Jesus wrestled with the horror of what he would go through but said 'Yes' for you. In what ways does this help you trust that God truly loves you?

10. What are the implications of grasping God's grace and accepting his love for your life on your frontlines?

Responding in Prayer

- Thank God for the true humanity we see in Jesus and for his loving obedience.

- Pray for one another and your responses to question 10.

- Ask God to bring to mind someone you'd love to draw closer to Jesus. In pairs, pray for these people, drawing on the insights of your discussion to shape your prayers.

The man who ran away

The young man in 14:51-52 is intriguing and his identity much discussed. Some traditions suggest he might even be Mark himself, an eyewitness to the events. However, he remains anonymous. Yet it was clearly important to Mark to note the man's part in the story. Jesus had predicted the failure of the disciples (14:27). Perhaps this young man represents the disciples who shamefully abandon Jesus rather than lay down everything to follow him.

JOY'S STORY

—

When Joy and her husband first moved to this city, they were 'just a passing through'. They'd always prayed that God would use them in their neighbourhood. After a while, they sensed he was calling them to settle in this one. So, they did, expectantly. As Joy put it, 'I believe that ordinary people are called to live extraordinary lives. Whenever I look in the face of another person, I know this is someone God loves and for whom Jesus has died. And I believe God may want to include me in his plans for them.'

As it happens, several older widowers live around the corner, and Joy often chats with them while out walking the dog. Over time, she noticed something about these men. Though always well attired, there was nevertheless something not quite right: a missing button, trouser legs an inch too short, a botched sewing attempt.

'I've always been a bit of a dab hand at sewing, and now that I'm retired, I've plenty of time to help people', she thought. So, she popped cards through the letterboxes of the 40 or so houses on the street, offering a free seamstress service.

Not long after, Ronnie, a short man with an infectious smile, got in touch. 'My daughter has just got her degree, and her graduation ceremony is happening upcountry in a few weeks. I really want to go, but my trousers don't fit very well at all.' 'Don't worry', consoled Joy, 'I'll pop round tomorrow at 10. Just have your trousers on inside-out and we'll get it sorted.'

She arrived the next day, pins in one hand, tape measure in the other, and got to work. As she was pinning up the hems, Joy noticed Ronnie's breathing. It sounded laboured and weak. 'Ronnie, your breathing really doesn't sound very good.' Then she asked him if he would like her to pray for him. Ronnie nodded.

Pins, needles, and the purposes of God

So, there they sat, Joy on the left of the sofa, Ronnie to the right, with trousers inside out, covered in pins. Before she prayed, Joy asked Ronnie if he believed Jesus could heal him. 'Yes, he can'. Then his voice weakened, 'But I'm not sure if I really believe in him.'

They spent the next little while talking about Jesus and then Joy guided Ronnie through a simple prayer. When she looked up, his cheeks were soaked in tears. 'Back when I was 14, I was in a Salvation Army Hall, because that's where I learnt to play the bugle. I heard people pray to accept Jesus into their lives, but for some reason, I never did it.' Some 70 years later, he finally did.

Ronnie made it to the graduation, feeling proud of his daughter... and his trousers. And over the coming months, Joy and her husband visited Ronnie and encouraged him in his faith.

One bright morning, Joy had barely left the garden path when she bumped into a neighbour who broke the news that Ronnie had passed away. Joy was gutted; she really loved him. But there was a comforting detail. 'When they found him, he was in a kneeling position next to his bed, with his hands folded as if he was praying.'

The gospel and its implications for all of life today

The gospel, Mark tells us, is the announcement of the good news about Jesus (1:1). So few words yet such catalytic impact. For Mark not only recounts *what* Jesus has done that changes the world forever, he reveals *how* and *why*. In so doing, Mark ignites our imagination for a rich and radical life with Jesus. He inspires our faith that God is powerfully present amongst his people. He increases our desire to live the way of Jesus wherever God places us in the world today. And he never hides the reality that it's probably going to be rather messy.

Key to all this is the way that Mark brings together both cross and kingdom to express the wholeness of the gospel message. The good news is about Jesus the longed-for Messiah, through whom God dealt decisively with evil and alienation. It's about Jesus the King. 'The time has come... The kingdom of God has come near. Repent and believe the good news!' Jesus declares (1:15). God reigns through King Jesus and whilst the fullness of this is still to be realised, God's power is at work in the world, amongst his people, by his Spirit.

Cross and kingdom are held together in Christ. Together they express the way of Jesus in the world. For the kingdom of God is the goal of God's purposes. This is the kingdom of God's *shalom*, when humanity and all creation will flourish with God in all their fullness. The cross is the way by which the kingdom of God comes. Diminishing either is to diminish the gospel. Both the Jesus-way of the cross and the Jesus-goal of the kingdom are necessary to live out the gospel and its implications for all of life today.

Cross-shaped kingdom possibilities
abound wherever we work and
live, study, worship, and play. They
abound in every sphere we may
relate to. They abound in the causes
God lays on our heart that reflect
his justice and mercy, his concern
for the poor, the broken, and the
marginalised. They abound in the
structures and systems, the politics
and cultures of our societies. They
abound amongst the people he's
placed us with — our families,
colleagues, friends, and neighbours.
They abound in the opportunities
to share this good news with
others. They abound in all of life,
and they abound all life long.

The gospel changes everything.
And we're invited to play our part.

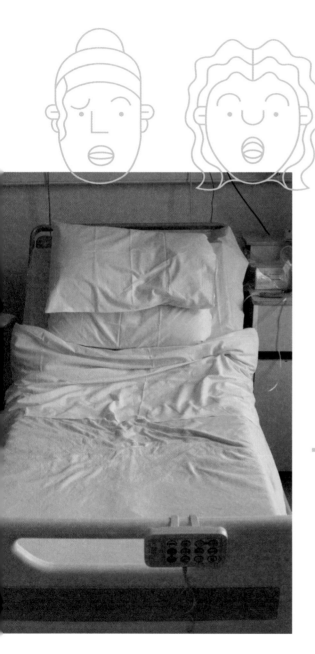

Session 6

Inviting Trust

Mark 16:1-8

First Thoughts

The Gospel of Mark ends with unusual abruptness. Views vary on whether Mark intended to finish at verse 8, whether he was unable to finish it for some reason, or whether his original ending has been lost in transmission. It's generally agreed, though, that the earliest recoverable form of Mark's Gospel ends at 16:8 and that 16:9-20 is not from the same author.

Beginnings and endings matter in a story. Echoing Genesis 1:1, Mark 1:1 signals a beginning no less momentous. Appearing suddenly on the scene, Jesus announces the joyful news that the kingdom is near. And now, at the end of Mark's Gospel, following Jesus' crucifixion, the young man in the tomb declares the astounding news: Christ is risen! The kingdom is launched. The regime has changed. God's re-creation of the world has begun.

It was a new beginning that took everyone by surprise, and it was decidedly messy. There's something in the abruptness of ending at verse 8 that helpfully reminds us of this. For that's the nature of kingdom life right now, in these in-between times. The kingdom has come; it's a present reality. And yet, the kingdom is still to come in all its fullness when every knee will bow before King Jesus. It's both exhilarating and something of a puzzle.

So, Mark ends with an implicit invitation: to trust Jesus who is alive and reigns; to give ourselves unreservedly to this new life in Christ which is so far from the triumphant life of a conquering king that most had imagined. Rather, we are to learn to live the way of Jesus in our context in our times, empowered by the same Spirit who raised him from the dead. Joyful news indeed!

Read – Mark 16:1-8

[1]When the Sabbath was over, Mary Magdalene, Mary the mother of James, and Salome bought spices so that they might go to anoint Jesus' body. [2] Very early on the first day of the week, just after sunrise, they were on their way to the tomb [3] and they asked each other, 'Who will roll the stone away from the entrance of the tomb?'

[4] But when they looked up, they saw that the stone, which was very large, had been rolled away. [5] As they entered the tomb, they saw a young man dressed in a white robe sitting on the right side, and they were alarmed.

[6] 'Don't be alarmed,' he said. 'You are looking for Jesus the Nazarene, who was crucified. He has risen! He is not here. See the place where they laid him. [7] But go, tell his disciples and Peter, "He is going ahead of you into Galilee. There you will see him, just as he told you."'

[8] Trembling and bewildered, the women went out and fled from the tomb. They said nothing to anyone, because they were afraid.

Focus on the Theme

1. Can you think of a time when your hopes were dashed? Briefly describe what it was like and how you felt.

What Does the Bible Say?

2. On the third day after Jesus' crucifixion the women went to the tomb. Their plan is described in 16:1-3. What does this suggest about what they were expecting?

Given Jesus' repeated advanced notices about what was going to happen (8:31; 9:31; 10:32-34; 14:27-28), are you surprised by their expectations and the absence of the other disciples at the tomb, or not?

3. What did the women see and experience in 16:4-5?

What was their reaction, and why?

4. What did the young man affirm (16:6-7)?

What did this mean, perhaps especially for Peter (14:66-72)?

5. Notice the women's confusion and fear in 16:8. In what ways does this reflect the disciples' responses to Jesus at times (4:41; 8:27-33; 9:6, 32; 14:50)?

Going Deeper

6. God's revolution has come, Jesus announced in 1:15. In what ways has Mark described Jesus as a radical throughout his Gospel?

How does the end of his Gospel fit with this?

7. Divide into three groups. Each group read one of the other Gospel accounts of the resurrection (Matthew 28:1-20; Luke 24:1-49; John 20:1-30). Compare and contrast Mark's account of the resurrection with these.

Living it Out ((o))

8. How does the fact of the resurrection shape the way you live on your frontline?

What would be different if it wasn't true?

9. Think about someone you've been praying for to draw closer to Jesus. In pairs, talk about how you would explain to them why you are a Christian.

10. The title of this guide is *Living the Way of Jesus in the World*. Considering Mark's Gospel, in what ways are you learning to trust Jesus on your frontline now?

Responding in Prayer

- Pray through your responses to question 10 together.

- Give thanks for the ways in which you have come to know Jesus more deeply through these sessions.

- Think about the people you have prayed for each session. Thank God for what he has done for each person and bless God's ongoing work in their lives.

- Read the Lord's Prayer slowly and silently (Matthew 6:9-13). Then pray it together.

Women as witnesses

All four Gospels report that women were the first witnesses to Jesus' resurrection and received the angel's commission to go tell the good news to the other disciples. This was deeply counter-cultural in Jesus' day. Women's testimony wasn't admissible in legal contexts. These women's testimony might not be considered an asset. Indeed, early pagan attacks on Christianity used the women's witness in their argument to dismiss the truth of the resurrection.

So, it's difficult to imagine the early church creating such a testimony unless they believed it to be true. Persuading the Jews to let go of their messianic expectations and embrace the unimagined reality of a dead and resurrected messiah would be a huge challenge. It didn't occur even to the disciples to check out the tomb on the third day, despite Jesus repeatedly telling them what would happen.

Messianic movements would come and go. It was the resurrection that restored the disciples' shattered hopes that God had indeed done a new thing. It was the resurrection that formed the heart of the good news about Jesus Christ, the Son of God (1:1), launching a revolutionary movement that changed the world forever. And it was women to whom this revelation of God was first entrusted.

Mark 16:9-20

Some believe that it was an accident that Mark's Gospel ends at verse 8. The original ending was somehow lost and never recovered through other copies in circulation. Another possibility is that Mark was prevented from finishing his Gospel, martyred perhaps. Still others are persuaded that the rather odd ending at verse 8 somehow fits the unexpected ending of the story itself and the consequent confusion of the disciples who struggled to quite know what to do with it all. Just as the first disciples were invited to put their trust in Jesus and work out the implications for his way in their times, so, too, are we invited to respond in faith.

Five different endings to Mark's Gospel have been preserved, none authored by Mark. In the longest of these (16:9-20), which appears in most manuscripts, we hear echoes of the other Gospels. Mary Magdalene is reported to be amongst the first witnesses. Jesus' appearance to the two travellers suggests the encounter with him on the road to Emmaus. His appearance to the Eleven recalls the disciples wrestling with doubt. And there are obvious echoes with Matthew's great commission and Luke's account of the ascension.

Most problematic is verse 18. In Acts 28:3-6, Paul is bitten by a poisonous snake yet is unharmed. But there's no account of drinking deadly poison with immunity in the New Testament. A late first-century cult involving poisonous drugs is reported to have exerted some influence on the early Christian community. The reference may be a suggestion that true Christian believers would be immune to such heresies.

Of course, the women did overcome their fear and passed on the news of what they'd seen and heard. For we have their testimony. The disciples did meet Jesus again. And the challenge to us remains: how will we respond to the extraordinary good news that Jesus is alive and goes ahead in taking the gospel of his kingdom wherever he calls us today?

Epilogue

At the end of this study of Mark's Gospel, try to find a time when you can review the whole study prayerfully before God.

_____

_____

_____

What was the most significant insight for you from the study?

_____

_____

_____

What did you learn about reading a Gospel?

_____

_____

_____

Looking back on what was happening on your frontline when you started, how have you seen God at work?

_____

_____

_____

Further reading on Mark

The following list offers some further reading on Mark for those who might like to dig deeper into the book.

Mark: A Commentary in the Wesleyan Tradition
New Beacon Bible Commentary
Kent Brower
Kansas City: Beacon Hill Press, 2012

Mark
The Story of God Bible Commentary
Timothy G. Gombis
Grand Rapids: Zondervan Academic, 2021

Mark
Tyndale New Testament Commentaries
Eckhard J. Schnabel
London: Inter-Varsity Press, 2017

Divine Government: God's Kingship in the Gospel of Mark
R. T. France
Vancouver, BC: Regent College Publishing, 2003

Other resources from LICC

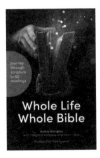

Whole Life Whole Bible

Whole Life Whole Bible
—

Walk through the story of the whole Bible in 50 readings and reflections and see how our lives are bound up with, and shaped by, God's plan to restore a broken universe. Far from restricting our faith to the 'personal' sphere, disengaged from everyday living, Scripture encourages us to take the Lord of life into the whole of life. It's a big story that forms our minds, fuels our imaginations, and fashions our daily lives as we live in God's world, in the light of God's word, wherever we are. Available in a book, email series, or YouVersion reading plan.

licc.org.uk/wholebible

Fruitfulness on the Frontline

LICC Website

We all have an everyday context that's significant to God, full of people who matter to God. But can we see how God might have been working in and through us on our frontlines? And can we imagine what more God might want to do there?

Brimming with real-life stories, biblical insight, and practical steps, these resources will spark your imagination and enrich your sense of wonder at the greatness and grace of the God who invites us to join his glorious work. The suite includes a book for individual reading and small group series including videos.

licc.org.uk/fruitfulness

Whether you're looking to grow in your understanding of the Bible and its implications for your daily life, how to respond to the pressures and opportunities in today's world or workplace, or looking for resources to help you as you lead a whole-life disciplemaking community, LICC's website is packed full of articles, videos, stories, and resources to help you on your journey. Sign up for weekly Bible reflections, blog posts, prayer journeys, and more.

licc.org.uk

About LICC

What difference does following Jesus make to our ordinary Monday to Saturday lives out in God's world? And how can we bring his wisdom, hope, grace, and truth to the things we do every day, to the people we're usually with, and the places we naturally spend time?

Vital questions in any era. After all, the 98% of UK Christians who aren't in church-paid work spend 95% of their time away from church, much of it with the 94% of our fellow citizens who don't know Jesus. Tragically, most Christians in the UK don't feel equipped to make the most of those opportunities. But what if they were?

That's what we at LICC are seeking to achieve. We work with individuals, church leaders, and theological educators from across the denominations. We delve into the Bible, think hard about the culture we're in, listen carefully to God's people, explore their challenges and opportunities... And we pray, write, speak, train, consult, research, develop, and test resources that offer the biblical frameworks, the lived examples, the practical skills, and the spiritual practices that enable God's people to know him more richly in their everyday lives, and grow as fruitful, whole-life followers of Christ right where they are, on their everyday frontlines, to the glory of God, and the blessing and salvation of many.

To find out more, including ways you can receive news of our latest resources, events, and articles, by email or post, go to licc.org.uk

licc.
The London Institute for
Contemporary Christianity